T0114186

THE PUB OF TRANSIENCE

A Collection of Poems and Haikus

G Damala

Trafford rev. 02/17/2011

 www.trafford.com

North America & international
toll-free: 1 888 232 4444 (USA & Canada)
phone: 250 383 6864 ♦ fax: 812 355 4082

Dedicated to my father, my late mother,
my late mother-in-law, and my beautiful wife.

Table of Contents

Poems

Las Vegas *1*

One More *2*

The Perfect Pint *3*

I Myself *4*

The First of Forever *5*

Let Yourself Go *7*

Morning Bus *8*

The Thunderstorm in the Distance *9*

A Morose Drinking Poem *10*

Atolls *11*

Drawn in the Sands *14*

Repose in a Mason Jar *15*

Singularity and the Heart *16*

Ode to George *17*

Late May Morning near Independence Bridge *20*

Disconnection *23*

The Arcadian Swan *24*

A Mid-January Midnight, in Shorts *31*

Hardships and Gifts *34*

Nothing Discerned *35*

What Do You Want to Do? *37*

I Will Be *39*

The Extent of Our Relationship *41*

My Apartment Floor *42*

Needs *43*

Or So I've Always Thought *45*

Poverty *46*

An April Evening in Budapest *47*

Two Women and I On a Bench at the Beach *49*

Public Libraries *51*

Untitled...54
Defining Moments 58
Narrowing It Down 59
New Year's Eve Realism...61
The View from the Circle Bar......................................65
Feeling and Sensitivity...67
A Window on Perspective...68
Entitlement...71
News of End 76
Deliquescence..77
Her Love 78
It's Best Experienced for Oneself...................................79
'Tis You..81
Fluttering 82
Contrast 83
One Look 84
A Body of Work...85
The Grain of Sand...86
Love Is a Binary Star System 87
The Pub of Transience...88
Encroaching Rhythms..90
Aroma of the World 91
Ourselves Lost 92
Damadola 93

A Collection of Haikus

Mood, Meditation, Gales, Time, Knowledge, Enlightenment.....97
Waiting, Foreplay, Coitus, Language, Languages, Soccer 98
Soccer 2, Beach, Beckonings, Fall, Conundrum, Release 99

Las Vegas

Las Vegas,
the glimmering desert jewel
with no conscience,
the place people seek
to run from their problems,
to flee themselves.
A den of heathens,
a kingdom
where one's
flaws, sins, and transgressions
are minimized and trivialized
by this iniquitous Hedon-opolis.
With money, motive, and mobility,
no sinner is too large or too evil
for this modern Babylon.
To cross lines
normally unthinkable to cross
is the lure:
no guilt, no reason, no excuse.
the perfect city to visit
if one be dishonest with
oneself,
because guilt,
to survive,
needs a conscience.

One More

Barley, malt, hops, and rice
with water combined
--such a wonderful vice
to my palate so kind.
On a hot summer eve
or a day so drab
I roll up my sleeve
and an iced one grab
(my world around
me is a mighty mess;
one more round or two
won't hurt, I guess).
It provides the will to live
or brings grateful pause.
The pleasure it doth give
from the strife it can cause.
The cold seductress,
she lulls me near
becomes my buttress
till I have no fear.
Then I sense the shame
early the next morn
as I fail the name
and avoid those eyes forlorn.
Oh, the paradox of beer
shakes me to the core
so tempting, so dear—
I think I'll have one more.

The Perfect Pint

I watched paradise cascade down the glass's side.
Then the phone rang.
She was calling after all this time.
Why?
Pain.
Her voice stopped my heart,
Drained my blood,
Closed my eyes.
I hung up. My heart restarted.
I sipped. My circulation resumed.
I opened my eyes.
No pain.
Perfect.

I Myself

What I seek
Is also
What I flee.
But
If I seek
What I flee
And
I flee
What I seek,
How will I ever be?

The First of Forever

An entrance
>Tender, soft, forgiving
Oh, so urgent
>Needful for living
Neural explosions
>Skin quite numb
Both hearts race
>So steady, a hum
Your mouth
>Open ever so slightly
Your gaze at me
>Ignites the North Sea
From a silky touch
>Chills down my spine
In your valley of honey
>I forever will dine
In sequence,
>Our bodies move as one
Our passionate embrace
>More intense than the sun
We shudder together
>The pace so slow
A cascade of pleasure
>Floods the vibrant meadow
I whisper your name
>For I dare not scream
To announce my ecstasy
>Dancing on a sunbeam
Paradise, I believe
>Could never this equal
Only a lifetime of this

With many a sequel
Would ever such feelings
        Begin to approach
So it is again
        This sweet act I will broach
There is no end
        As we embrace forever
The circle will continue
        In perpetual endeavor
Yes, thee I love with
        Full body, heart, and soul
My much better half
        Because of whom I now am whole
For this, and for you,
        I am truly blessed
And to you and us
        You will have my infinite best.

Let Yourself Go

Toss them out the door
Feel your lusty ambitions to your very core
Relax, enjoy, and trust in our love
For I fit into you like a silken glove
Our skin, our bodies, our passion
Let them engulf you in such a fashion
As to realize your fantasies and desires
Let the dreams of eroticism light your fires
I am your lover, your partner, your one
Let yourself go, be woman, and run...

Morning Bus

Morning bus
Why art thou my thorn?
No place to rest my arm
And my seat is so worn
Would it be too much harm
To have, like all the rest,
A hook to hang my coat?
I loathe to be a pest
Or grumpy as a goat
But I to thee do direct
Some more thoughts of mine:
My seat won't stay erect
And the jolts hurt my behind
Why can't you stay on keel
And be a ride so smooth?
When we're through, I'll fall to kneel
My fears and frights to soothe
Then at thee I will look
And think of earlier morn
Oh, ye bus, fulsome crook
Why art thou my thorn?

The Thunderstorm in the Distance

Small and inconsequential
against a backdrop of
precipices, crevices, wildlife, and rocks,
a running chipmunk tips over
a small stone
and the echo sounds alone
as it travels hundreds of feet
down to its next place of rest.
Down below, a small cliff is visible,
where one can sit and dangle one's legs,
listening to the din of silence
from that cliff.
One can also see a distant desert thunderstorm,
hear Jim Morrison's poetry,
feel the ghosts of earlier visitors
blowing in the wind,
or look at the gathering of cirrus and cumulus
to imagine faces, animals, dreams, lovers.
A shadow crosses the distinct canyon floor below,
like that which crosses one's face
at the thought of being
so small and inconsequential.

A Morose Drinking Poem

My wife has left,
my life's bereft,
I don't feel like going out.
I'll stay inside,
my time I'll bide,
While drinking Guinness Stout.

Atolls

I push and I pull
while wisps of smoke
waft lazily through rock
and hurried millings go by.
Unmoved, I move to a place where
shade is my light,
green is my shelter,
and squeals from Nature – not Humanity –
are my music;
where feet replace tires,
pulp replaces metal,
the sky is leafy green,
the ground beneath is dirt not litter,
and the smell that clings to me
isn't tired and noxious
but alive and unmistaken.
The pull and push
become sedated and lulled
in the serene answer of Nature
to my frantic call for sanity.
Life ambles by,
hopping on three-clawed feet,
fluttering with the rhythm of air,
flapping its transparent wings,
or crawling along my cracked skin.
I am envious:
there is no push and pull
within this realm,
just a straightforward
search for survival –
simple, instinctive, unfettered.

Sentience raises me to a
viewpoint above theirs,
yet lowers me to a
thanklessness below.
With this in mind,
I conjure up a familiar line,
paraphrased herewith:
no one is an island unto oneself,
but each of us is and becomes more so
as we lose sight of what is simple,
of what is glorious,
of what is kind,
of what is alive:
how trees lean to and fro,
how pistils bend under pollen's burden,
how leaves murmur when wind beckons,
how snails fall in love,
how creeks shape the rocks,
how feathers flutter.
Yet, as the gulfs between us
grow into oceans,
we become acrid and hostile,
hospitably malicious,
rendered without oases
in an ever-expanding desert
untenable for growth,

parched for love,
thirsting for emotion,
desperate for desire,
seeking truth; and,
in the end,
there is a hole inside us
that dominates,
where we are no longer
islands,
but are far worse:
atolls,
which lack what is necessary
to be fully above the surface;
instead, death comes in an immersion
of what is omnipresent
and unwavering,
where, without a center,
without a middle,
all caves in.
And all that exists
is a vacuum,
where there is
no push and no pull.

Drawn in the Sands

Revelations hit me in waves
then fade like a tan.
I struggle to be consistent
but am hindered
by a lack of control,
my own boundaries,
drawn in the sands of
unimaginative creativity
that the winds of sentience
blow askew in my fleshy deserts.
A red tide engulfs me,
rendering my platitude
unconscious.

More revelations ensue:
I am a puppet to them.
Even as I fight their
attempts at mastery,
I want to master them.
The cycle is eternally finite –
neverending but never the same.
I crave shelter
where I am immersed
in inebriation,
its sloped angles of protection,

comforting me,
blinding me,
nurturing me,
strengthening me,
raising me,

razing me.

Repose in a Mason Jar

Two toothbrushes repose
In a Mason jar in the bathroom,
A sign of separation and distance.
Each is yang to the
Distant toothbrushes of yin,
Breaking what is harmonious and essential.
The pain and loneliness are severe,
Slowing the heart rate, yet pumping the blood,
Numbing the nerves and piercing the soul to its
core.
The sweet nectar of completeness is
Now a bitter vintage of emptiness.
Balance is absent and the evenness is odd;
A lack of coldness absorbs the warmth,
Leaving a vacuum of color that
Pales and distorts all that remains.

Singularity and the Heart

The heart is a tattered warrior,
hitchhiking sporadically,
leading, following, pausing, skipping.
It tries to lead the man,
but often loses its influence on him
because of a disconnected mind
that tries too hard to be something
it isn't
or tries too hard to deny what really
it is.

Left alone, to act on its own volition,
the heart pulses with a resonating allure,
for deep inside lie unknown depths of
compassion, love, warmth, and strength.
It is pure, unsullied by society,
Untouched by the erosion of experience,
Unfazed by the gentle persuasiveness
Of pedantry.

The singular heart accomplishes and
Forges its own paths, creates its own landscapes.
Its mysteries are benevolent and revered;
It is to be treated respectfully, justly,
Without negative interference from the
Scarred and equally mysterious mind.
The intelligent man must obey its whims,
Heed its demands,
And answer its calls.

Ode to George

Father George, how great is your reach.
Here I am, humble squid, sitting
on a small grassy Hungarian knoll
admiring Heroes' Square in the bright May sun
with you peering over my shoulder.
I am nothing;
       but because of you,
I am someone,
I am free,
I am fortunate,
a state of being my fellow countrymen
do not appreciate here at millennium's end.
Your courage, bravery, leadership,
     even your apple tree,
have made sure that our
       stars and stripes
have always been and
       always will be;
and have made possible a freedom
which is taken for granted in your homeland,
but which the world over
is sought by so many
          less fortunate,
envied by those
        not allowed to have
   it,
despised by those
        too weak to understand
   it,
feared by those
        too obtuse to accept
   it.

The free and the brave has become a land besieged
between the familiar shores and as well as abroad.
It is becoming a land of shackles and cowards.
Dishonesty
—not a young George—
is wielding a sharp blade
on the tree of American harmony and integrity,
each swing further severing the foundation
of character you laid over two centuries ago.
Self-interest is the only thing
        self-evident today;
Not peace, not faith,
not unity as Americans –
Not even unity for America.
You set us free, and free we remain –
        from external forces.
But it is decay from within that gives me pause
and freezes me like your likeness behind me:
children gunning down children;
politicians twisting your words
        to benefit themselves;
muckrakers promoting their own interests;
hatemongers thrusting their poison upon the
ignorant.

There is
a shedding of responsibility,
      an exodus from patriotism,
            a loosening of one's bonds from friends
and family,
          a retreat from the right of privacy,
          a loss of innocence.
We need a voice, a beacon, direction,
        a 21st-century clone of you,
not afraid of mistakes,
        not afraid of honesty,
to stabilize our shaky foundation.
I wonder where he or she might be?
I wonder if anyone else cares on a level
        not motivated by self-gains?

Oh, Father George, how great is your reach?

Late May Morning near Independence Bridge

To my left a hard bench is the soft mattress
Of a homeless drunk.
Above me hangs a hazy, mid-morning sun,
Delivering its yet-unlocked gifts.
Beneath my feet are stones and shells of cigarette
butts
Instead of fine grains of sand.
To my right, a kindly old woman sits:
She asks in a language I don't understand
to borrow my pen: I give it to her.
Behind me, lumbering metal buses
Screech, squeal, lurch, and bellow reproachfully as
A slight breeze ruffles the skin
Of my visible, hairless head.
The smell of the swollen nearby river
gently envelops me,
Then is rudely abducted
by the careless exhaust of traffic.
All around me, people hurry to their destinies
While I sit and ascribe mine.
A busload of school children rides by and waves at
me,
Curious *tablae rasae*, their whole lives in front of
them.
I smile and wave back.

A hundred meters or so away,
A big green bridge looms silently,
Lending an austerity to what I see.
Its grand presence, replete with
Iron eagles, spires, rivets, knobs, national emblems,
and history,
Gives pause to all the commotion surrounding it.
It stands freely, boldly, resolutely,
As it has for decades,
The blood of sacrifice that gave it its name
Able to be felt if one looks or listens closely
enough.
And although a liege to the raging Danube below,
Guarding the principles of the water it spans,
Connecting the people that the water separates,
it keeps its balance, maintains its strength,
Symbolic, historic, patriotic, emphatic,
A testament to scruples, courage, and freedom.

To my left,
stirred by the sun's warmth,
The drunk sits up,
While the sun, having shed its hazy yoke, now
Hovers sternly and purposefully
Over the stones and butts that are still beneath my
feet instead of sand.

To my right,
no longer does the kindly old woman sit and
Ask, in a language I don't understand,
To borrow my pen.
The sounds of the buses are now intermittent, yet
consistently reproachful.
The breeze intensifies its efforts to ruffle my still
hairless head and
I am rudely assaulted by the smell of exhaust,
Which then gives way
to the wonderfully earthy smell of the river.
New pursuers of destiny hurry by me now,
As do ingenious thoughts that I should write
down.
The school children on the passing tour bus
Have long since departed and with them go
My high hopes of a bright future for Central
Europe.
I stand and walk home.

Disconnection

The cork from the nearly empty bottle
Lies on the stone floor,
Looking up at the effect its disconnection
From its former glass home has upon
The pen racing across the paper.

It wonders about its purpose, its reason
For where it is and where it was.
Is it responsible for the words,
Whether ingenious or obtuse,
Splashed across the wine-splotched paper?

Lying on the floor, its usefulness has passed,
But its effect is potentially eternal.
It wonders if the ruby tinge on its body
Symbolizes its stain of culpability?

Scared, nervous, its conscience burdened,
The cork lies silently, cursing its lack of
Dexterity, lack of control, and its lot in life.
It is unable to cleanse and absolve itself
Of what may come.

The Arcadian Swan

Walking, wooden spear clutched in hand,
An unknown angel of the land,
One of huntress Diana's girls,
Ties up her hair to hide its curls.
In faithful rhythm doth she step
Doing her duty with great pep.
A virgin girl so pure and chaste
Had no man yet been given taste.
Her fair honey, such sweet nectar,
Would weaken even Prince Hector.
She wore not her dress in lewd style;
Nor were her actions wanton and vile.
No, this swan of Arcadia,
Most very dear to Trivia
Was full of hope and did no wrong.
Yet no one's power lasts for long!

Once, gliding down an unworn path,
Jupiter did toward his bath
Spot on a knoll, where there did lay
Resting, one bright and sunny day,
Our fair maiden, unsuspecting.
For how would she be expecting
That in an unknown place as this
There'd be lurking her vestal kiss?
And this would be no normal buss,
For if discovered, such a fuss
Would be raised --in envious ire.
And into straits divinely dire
By jealous Juno she'd be cast
Yea, such action would be her last.

For Jupiter, lascivious,
To our sweet swan 'twas obvious
What he should do; damn the fury
Of his wife, for there was no jury
Who'd punish him or quoth his guilt:
He'd not suffer for Juno's jilt.

Quite beautiful, our swan asleep,
That with one glance, most men would weep
And before her, kneel in stark praise.
But to mortals what doth them faze
To the great gods there is no such
Just feeling good, a lusty touch.
Thus, did Jupiter, in disguise
Approach our swan full of lies,
"I ask of thee, my dear minion.
Upon which, in your opinion,
Of these mountains would you seek
The sexual pleasures of the weak?"
Such a question from the goddess
Would ne'er cross her lips so modest.
But dear Callisto –that's our swan—
Did not catch the god's shrewd con.
For his disguise as the huntress
Was so real, she'd no cause for unrest.
"Oh my goddess, to thee I hail.
If you'd ask, I'd all the seas sail.
As there is no other above
You, my Diana, that I love:
Vesta, Venus, even Juno
Nor Jove, Mars, or all those we know."

Smile, did Jupiter, at this claim,
Glad to hear Artemis above his name.
Then he reached out and pulled her near.
Those screams and cries, no one could hear
As Callisto fought with all her might.
And had she seen our swan's brave fight
Juno's rage would have rescinded
On our swan would have descended
Not her ire, so vengeful and great.
Alas, 'twas not Callisto's fate
For what girl can fight off a god?
Jupiter left her where he'd trod.
To the skies he, afterward, flew.
Burdened felt she, as grass by dew.
The sly, watching woods did mock her
And like from Pandora's locker
The plagues let loose on man to tread
She from her shame hastily fled.

As she soon rejoined the ranks,
Diana called out to say thanks
For being so honest and pure.
Words like this our swan thought a lure
By Jupiter again to trap
And seduce her into his lap.
But Callisto, our troubled swan,
Saw the goddess and nymphs go on.
So she joined, eyes averted
Thinking now her life perverted.
'Twas hard for her to hide her face
Of guilt, so she lessened her pace,

No more one of Diana's first,
Shamed, her body about to burst.
These signs the goddess did not heed
Although the nymphs knew the bad weed
Taking hold in our swan's pure soul,
Replacing her heart a deep hole.

Soon, the orbed moon again waxed nine
The weary clan stopped to recline,
Tired from the hunt, tired from the run
As hot upon them shone the sun.
In cool woods from her brother's heat
Did Diana find for their feet
A fresh, Elysian sapphire spring.
"Let us naked swim, bathe, and sing,"
Did Artemis joyfully cry.
"For no man's here on us to spy."
At this, did our Callisto blush
As to disrobe the others did rush
And to enjoy the bubbling brook.
Our swan recalled Jupiter's rook
And to disrobe did she alone
Decline, her feet from shame like stone.
Her delay was to no avail:
They stripped her bare and let out a wail
At the sight of her full with child.
Diana yelled, our swan reviled
"Leave! Go Away! From here depart!
You bring ignominy, you tart,
To this, our pure and virtuous flock.
By your actions, do us you mock!

I, from this clique, do thee expel!"
This to our swan was a death knell.

Yet for Callisto there was more:
"You have wronged me, you little whore,"
From Juno came these brutal words
More fatal the sharp claws of birds
Could not have been than the revenge
As Juno sought to cruelly avenge
The shame upon her that'd been cast
By her husband's carnal repast.
"You flirt, from thee I'll freely take
What beguiled my husband's lusty ache:
The beauty that so you pleases!
Learn to desist your racy teases!"
With that, she seized our fair swan's hair
And to the ground, arms in prayer,
Callisto, suppliant, was hurled,
As Juno's anger flew unfurled.
Callisto's arms began to bristle
With long black hair thick as thistle
While fingers became long curved claws
And hands bent into large black paws.
Her face, once a cherub's pleasure,
Became then an unsightly treasure
Upon whose eyes there'd land a curse
If at her a glance would not reverse.
Her power of speech did she lose;
No cries for mercy could she use.
Only now was a forlorn growl,
Combining with a mournful howl,

To replace her once-pleasing song.
So she took her place in among
The other creatures of the wood
Running with those she thought were good
Once when the forest was her home
And through the trees she'd freely roam.
Become afraid, did she to sleep
Under shade, she would nightly weep.
Pursued o'er hills by baying hounds,
Hills that once were her hunting grounds.
Once, upon a vile mirrored stare
She hid herself from its like glare.
Her life became a vast ruin
Our lovely swan, now a bruin.

Some years later, a strong young lad
Named Arcas, in hunting gear clad
When in the wood he did but see
A she-bear ogling him strangely.
He ran away, afraid the beast
Might take him for her dinner feast.
She from his sight ne'er took her gaze
Even as he at her did raise
A spear with which to drive her through.
But who should come to her rescue?
Why Arcas's father, of course:
God of all, and full of remorse
At near-matricide by his spawn.
Jupiter lifted to the dawn
Both, on a gently blowing breeze,
Mother and son with utmost ease.

In the heavens, placed side by side,
Now they brighten the eventide,
Creating twin constellations
Giving us illuminations:
Callisto, now major Ursa
And Arcas, yes, minor Ursa.

A Mid-January Midnight, in Shorts

Midnight
in mid-January
sitting in shorts
on a bench at the corner of
Santa Monica and Wellesley.
Across Santa Monica Boulevard
          (straight ahead)
is Rocky's hot dogs and hamburgers.
Across Wellesley
                              (to my right)
is Del's Saloon,
into which I have set foot many times.
A perspiring can of Coors
sits next to me
(to my left)
and keeps me company
as I watch the sparse traffic meander by.
I think about my
being in shorts
at midnight
in mid-January
(it is Los Angeles, after all)
and it brings to mind
where I was a year ago
(Budapest)
and two years ago
(Boulder),
neither in which place
I'd be sitting outside
at midnight
in shorts
in mid-January.

I watch the traffic
and enjoy the night.
A Lexus, a Honda, a Chrysler
all drive by;
then a Ford pickup truck
and several other cars.
However, my mind is not there on the bench;
no, it thinks about
my soon-to-be ex-Mrs.
in bed at home:
a second marriage failure.
I feel pathetic and I'm not even
thirty-two years old yet.
I am momentarily brightened at the thought
of two potential successors, though:
one in Hungary
and one in Turkey.
But I've a feeling they would just be
the third and fourth ex-Mrses,
so I decide not to take my act
international just yet.
Hell, they probably aren't even
potential suitors;
it's probably just
the Coors talking or
the desire for good drama amidst all
this rubbish.

Questions do remain, though,
and chances saunter past me
like the traffic in front of me.
Perhaps, however,
as I am doing with these cars,
I am merely watching great chances pass by me.
I get up to walk home and I walk past Del's.
It's definitely a bar I know well and will only
know better, and, although I know
it would certainly be OK in mid-June or -July,
I wonder if it would be OK for me to be inside
sitting in shorts
at midnight
in mid-January.

Hardships and Gifts

Often, I am as tired of life's
       gifts
as I am sick of life's
       hardships,
for recriminating strings
are often attached to the
       gifts
while bombast and circumstance
often accompany the
       hardships.

Nothing Discerned

The glass of beer looks at me.
I struggle for words,
for what it is I feel.
Seven weeks of blurred senses
that were numbed by the holidays
has just passed
--no escape from the madness.
I've put on weight,
lost my sense of time,
and abandoned my purpose.
Ideas seep in and out like the tide,
only the landscape of my brain has
not became smooth and level.
I read Bukowski, Fante, Dostoevsky,
in search of direction, but I discern nothing.
A song on the tape player comes on
--a bald woman is singing and I am reminded
of a college roommate who really
liked her music.
This roommate's name was Jacob
and thinking of Jacob
saddens me,
for I have wasted time, talent, and tangency.

More than a decade has passed:
one ex-Mrs. and another one soon to be,
travels all around this country
and to two other continents,
neither enough carnal knowledge
nor alcohol
have I had the fortune to encounter,
only too much judgment and too little openness,
at once hypocritical and extreme,
while running from myself
and from being loved.
Fear is my guardian,
yet I use boastfulness to cower from it.
Anger is a fissionable component
that doesn't mix well with Insecurity.
But it all is an endless cycle from which
I cannot emerge.
So, I look at the glass of beer
looking at me
and I struggle for words
and for what I feel.

What Do You Want to Do?

People ask
        but I don't know.
People asked
        and I didn't know then.
People will ask
        but I still won't know.
If I could,
        I would travel, write, drink, and read.
Then I would
        drink and write about what I'd read
        and where I had travelled.
While drinking and writing,
        I'd think about what to read
        and where to travel next.
While travelling and reading,
        I'd write and think about
        where I would drink next.
It would be an intimate cycle
        of travelling, drinking, writing, and reading,
           or
        of drinking, writing, reading, or travelling
           or
        any single, double, triple, or quadruple
        combination of the above.

But, G, one might ask
        what about women?
        Where do they fit into your picture of life?
Would you do any kissing
or loving or chasing
or grabbing or what?
Oh, believe me, I'd answer,
women would be on my mind,
alright,
Hell, I'd say, they're the reason I'd be
        travelling,
        writing,
        reading,
                and
        drinking,
trying
to run from and run toward,
to describe what I'd had and I'd want,
to learn why they've been and why they will be,
to remember and to forget.

I Will Be...

I will be the truth
    when you need honesty
I will be the warmth you seek
    when you grow cold
I will be the lean-to under which you huddle
    when escaping the tempest
I will be the one who plucks the burr from your heel
    when you go barefoot
I will be the moon's luminescence
    when your world darkens
I will be the vodka
    when your cranberry juice needs a kick
I will be the bear hug that comforts you
    while you sleep
I will be the soap and water
    that washes the dirt from your skin
I will be the baby's breath
    that complements your dozen roses
I will be the one who holds your hand
    when you cross the street
I will be your nourishment
    when you are famished
I will be with you
    when you cannot see me
I will be the inkwell
    when your plume runs dry
I will be the delicate brush
    that colors your nails
I will be the blue-green eyes
    that gaze into yours
I will be the fortunate grains of sand underneath
    when you recline to sunbathe

I will be the strong hands
    that unknot your tension
I will be the ring
    that enwraps your finger
I will be the keeper
    of your fears and pains
I will be the pillow on which your head lies
    when you rest
I will be the earth holding you
    when you put down roots
I will be the hot water
    that dilutes your coffee to perfection
I will be the soft caress
    that makes you shudder breathlessly
I will be the one who watches
    when you try on clothes
I will be the sentry
    who ensures you sleep well
I will be the one to whom you turn
    when you're in a time of need
I will be the ear
    when you need to vent
I will be the man
    who reminds you that you are all woman
I will be the man
    who accepts nothing less than you
I will be the man
    who wants nothing more than you
Whatever you want me to be
    I will be...

The Extent of Our Relationship

I once tried to buy beer after 11 p.m.
on a weeknight in a grocery store
on Wilshire in West Los Angeles.
A simple thing, I thought.

I was sober, thirsty,
        and I didn't have to work the next day.
        My mood was anticipatory as I strode
        to the counter with a 12-pack of Coors.

        However, the clerk said, apologetically,
"Maybe you don't know,
        but we can't sell alcohol
        after eleven o'clock on weeknights."

        Dumbfounded, I walked home,
        grabbed a bottle of whiskey
from which I'd been trying to hide
        and sat down in the recliner, no glass.

        My wife watched all of this
        and then asked, "I thought you
        went to get beer?"
        "I did," I replied, and opened the bottle.

"Well, what happened?"
"They don't sell it past 11 during the week."
"So, you're gonna drink whiskey instead?"
"Yep."

She got up and went to bed.

My Apartment Floor

Almost every day, I grouse
about my restlessness and laziness
and how, in America,
my creativity and initiative
suffer because of these.
I am mesmerized here in the States
by all the vacuous choices available,
yet, I do nothing to improve my lot.
Instead of reading or writing,
things I love most to do,
I surf the Internet.
Instead of sitting in a bar with character,
I sit in one that serves fruity drinks
          and has a neon sign.
Instead of walking and admiring
that which is around me,
I drive everywhere,
          staring only at traffic.
Instead of sitting in a park
or strolling on the beach,
I loll on my apartment floor
          like a beached walrus.
And just when I think it can't get worse,
right now, I am sitting on the floor
          of my apartment,
waiting for the cable guy
          to come install my cable TV.

Needs

"Do you know an
empty garage
I could use?
That's all I need,
just a small one,"
he said.

I looked at what Manuel was wearing --
shabby shoes
worn trousers,
white t-shirt,
turqoise polo shirt,
a brown tweed sportcoat;

and his Von's
grocery cart
full
of his meager
possessions:

a blanket,
a second pair of trousers,
a spare sportcoat,
and two or three boxes
full
of his papers and notes--

and was
thunderstruck
at the frugal
statement
of his simple needs.

I became
ashamed
at all I wanted
and thought
I needed.

Or So I've Always Thought

Attitude
is something
chosen,
not inherited
(or so I've always thought).
Yet, I notice
many people with bad
attitudes
and I wonder
why they've chosen to be
that way.
By my reckoning,
I'd figure that most people
would choose a good
attitude,
to be happy.
But having a good
attitude
takes a bit of work
and requires
selflessness,
and
we live in
a selfish
and
lazy
society.

Poverty

Today, while walking down
Wilshire Boulevard,
I saw a nun driving a luxury car
--an Infiniti, I believe.
Some vow of poverty, I thought,
as thirty meters away
lay an old homeless man
whose luxury car was a
Von's grocery cart.

An April Evening in Budapest

It was one night in April
when my homeboy Luke and I
got into it
about poetry.

Both of us had pent-up aggression that night—
the result of our women—
as we stumbled down the street, drunk.
He berated me for liking and admiring
Keats, Wordsworth, and Shelley,
and for trying to write like they did
--in meter and tempo and rhyme.
"Come on, Goltz," I responded,
"to write well in rhyme and verse
takes talent.
Writing in free verse
is too easy;
any schmuck can do that."

He glared at me, offended,
You see, all he wrote was free verse.

We kept walking—staggering—
punch-drunk from going toe-to-toe
with a group of
muscle-bound Warsteiner pints
that had unsuspectingly jumped us
in some small dive bar.

After a few moments,
Goltz laid into me:

"You are so pretentious
and goddamned contentious."

I couldn't disagree,
And, really, I had
No energy to do so.

But I did start writing free verse from that moment
on.

Two Women and I On a Bench at the Beach

I am sitting on
a bench at the beach
listening to
two gabby women.

I am listening on
a bench to two gabby women
sitting on
the beach.

I am two gabby women
listening to
a bench
sitting at the beach.

I am the beach
listening to
two gabby women
sitting on a bench.

I am a bench
sitting on the beach
listening to
two gabby women

Two beach women
sitting on a gabby
listening to the bench--
I am.

Two gabby women
listening to
a bench at the beach
I am sitting on.

Public Libraries

Speaking to a
homeless person
may engage you in one of the
most
intellectual conversations
you have ever had
because they
may be the
most
well-read people in America.
Laugh, if you want,
but check out
the number of
homeless people
sitting in public libraries
reading
and check out
whom they are probably
reading:
Rushdie, Pound, Hemingway,
Vonnegut, Dostoevsky;
and about what they are probably
reading:
politics, SETI, sociology, color codes, philosophy,
conspiracy theories,
survival.
G, you say,
I don't usually go to public libraries,
so I wouldn't know.

Well, I know you don't go—
most
people don't anymore.
Corporate bookstores
have joined with
corporate coffeehouses
to relegate the need for public libraries
to high school students and
homeless people.
Look at the facts and one understands:
       corporate has mobile phones
       public has pay phones;
       corporate has double mocha decaf latte
       public had fluoridated water;
       corporate has millions in advertising
       public has millions in overdue charges;
       corporate smells like prime wealth
       public smells like the grime of life;
       at corporate, people check out
each other's looks
       at public, people check out
authors' books;
       and corporate has stories by unseen people
           discussing their perspectives of life
       while public has the actual perspectives of life
           sharing a reading table with you.
Homeless people
give their stories without want of
financial recompense;
they merely seek an ear to bend,
a touch of humanity,
someone to listen.

Public
is a place unafraid of itself,
in touch with its residents,
open to those seeking
knowledge,
a card catalogue,
reference,
or even shelter.
It is here that
one can
read, breathe, formulate, gather.
It is here that
homeless people
slough off the stenched burnoose
of shame and non-acceptance
forced upon by society
like a father's hand upon a helpless child's cheek.
It is here that
they have
access to what
most
of us take for granted:
feeling like
a real
person,
part of the world.
respectable,
not ignored.

Untitled

A country built on democracy and capitalism
a place where all voices can be expressed
a chance for all to make a living
by any means necessary.
The Great Melting Pot
is the country's proud moniker.
E pluribus unum
a saying on all the currency,
repeated in oaths,
in one form or another,
a forgotten citation
as the voices of those in minority
rise and rise in volume
threatening the very concepts of authority.
The lure of competition, capitalism,
the lust for money, to be the best,
denigrate the foundation of the country.
The democracy lessens as the competitive idea
blossoms, threatening the core.

We hide behind a mantra of
'political correctness' and look down upon
the tenets upon which the country was constructed.
We are losing the grip on reality, on how to live,
on what is right, on what is veracious.

We litigate when things go not as desired;
we go behind the backs of
brothers and sisters in order
to increase or improve ourselves;
how we look, what we possess, where we live,
all counting for more than how we act;
we complain about our plights even
as we refuse to help those more in need;
our myopia overwhelms our conscience
and we act not true to what is right,
but, instead, true toward what will be thought of us.

We are afraid to be, stand, or think alone,
because it is perceived to be a flaw
and who wants a flaw to be exposed in this era?
Our fight for and celebration of the independence
we have is now laughable as we have become a nation
of malcontent co-dependents, unaccountables,
fence-sitting opportunists,
on the ready for our neighbor's misstep
so we can raise ourselves up.
We are losing sight of what is right and what is wrong
as we instead focus on a label or ideology that is
misapplied or misused or misfocused.

We stand for morality even as we live immorally;
we judge others even as we lash out at being
judged;
we have lost our simplicity as our
technology advances to dizzying heights;
we think of ourselves as the Creators or Improvers
of all that is around us in Nature and the Universe;
we see differences
instead of noticing similarities;
we hear what we want to hear
instead of listening;
we reach for what we think is ours
instead of feeling what others feel;
we lift our noses in the air at others less fortunate
instead of smelling the decay of society;
we stick our tongues out at what we don't understand
instead of tasting the incredible delights others offer;
we take what we want
instead of sharing what we have.

We consider ourselves the leaders of the world,
the nation to which many
others look for guidance and emulation,
yet we are not worthy of the responsibility,
a responsibility upon which some of the major
foundations of this nation were erected.
We have taken this load for granted and
have used it to bully our way into the lives of others.

Slowly, but increasingly, other countries are
hoping to find another alternative to the bullying.
But, they are in the unfortunate position
of being at our mercy when negotiating with us.
So, we take advantage of our strength,
forcing our views upon the rest of the world.
We have sanctions against certain countries because
we have taken it upon ourselves to morally police
these countries because of their repugnant leaders,
many of whom
are not even the choice of the people they lead.
So, we cause so much anguish because of our
policing of countries and their leaders where
it should not be our business to police;
we too often take our role as world leader
further than it needs to be taken and we lose
sight of what is really being accomplished
by these actions:
the sufferings of millions and millions of innocents.

Defining Moments

A moment can be defining
       when in the event of
a moment's happening,
But a moment is not defined
       until after the event of
a moment's happening,
Thus, we cannot define what a
       moment means when
a moment's happening.

Narrowing It Down

Choices.
What are choices?
Why do we have them?
Should we be allowed to have them?
I have heard that they open us up
to the many possibilities that exist
and that they encourage us to make
decisions,
and sometimes we
have to make tough decisions,
which is good for us,
makes us better men, better women, better people.
To hell with that, I say.
I don't want choices that only make me feel better;
I also want choices that make me feel good,
like Tupac or Biggie
whiskey or tequila,
blonde or redhead,
eating or penetrating,
right breast or left,
futbol or hockey,

Bukowski or Miller,
mountains or seas.
These aren't choices that necessarily
make us better people, or
build our character, or
mold our minds;
but they are choices that make us
happy,
        drunk,
aroused,
        orgasmic,
fortunate,
        well-read,
content.
Frost said all the difference was
the one less travelled by.
I take the one that makes me feel good
with no regrets.
You see, narrowing it down to choices
without regrets
makes all the difference to me.

New Year's Eve Realism

I don't write much on
        love and romance these days.
Both are emotions to which
        I cannot relate very well
and have seemingly denigrated
        in my failed relationships.
But I want not to whine
        or make this a bitter song.
No, I am a romantic
        to my very core --believe it or not.
As much as I've wanted
        to treat it with realism,
the mistake has been in
        my shameful idealizing of it.
I've put it on a pedestal
        --too high for my reach--
instead of rising up
        to look it in the eye.
I've wanted it to consume me,
        and often it has.
Unfortunately, its consummation
        of me wore off after a short time,
leaving me disgruntled,
        disappointed, and dissatisfied.
Too often I strove for it
        to martyr or glorify me
when I should have allowed it
        to complement me.

We are taught to expect
        romance to be idealistic,
which, yes, it can be;
        too often, however, the realistic
part of romance is ignored
        when we are taught it,
leaving us quite unprepared
        for the demands of love's rigors.
Thus, we lack the commitment
        to ride through the valley of realism
until the momentum of it all carries
        us upward to that zenith of idealism.
We forget the tender caress
        when we see the sag or wrinkle.
We avoid the loving embrace
        when we notice the extra girth.
We disregard the fiery kiss
        when those lips say something inane.
We ignore the moon's reflection in the eyes
        that might fail to notice us as they once did.
We don't remember the skin's sweet smell
        when life's weather begins to take its toll.
We fail to run hands through hair
        that now is not as lustrous or bountiful.
We don't take time to properly love the body
        that once fired us beyond molten.

We overlook how we once touched
        as our stresses from the world mount.
We disdain the aura of candlelight
        for the harsh luminescence of fluorescence.
We neglect the love before us because
        we think we seek that which we're led to
believe we seek.
Commitment is lost in a world of
        desensitization and overstimulation.
People lament technology's ability
        to reveal our infidel indiscretions
when, instead, people should lament
        its ability to lure our emotions astray.
In the end, one should remember
        that love is relative
and not just for individuals who are searching,
        or for individual couples,
but also for the individuals
        who make up those couples.
Love should be respected and nurtured
        each point of view given a chance.
The bad and good side of love
        should be communicated, not hidden.
It should not be unjust, but fair.
        It will hurt, but it shouldn't demean.
It should be passionate and warm,
        not cold and apathetic.

It should be given with instinct and ease,
      for only then can it thus be returned so.
It should be met with breathless expectation
      and not with hopeless fear.
It should be anticipated and awaited,
      not humiliating and emasculating.
It should not be used as a weapon,
      it should be something beautiful wept on.
We need to appreciate and respect it,
      be honest with and obeisant toward it.
If we aren't, I fear it will lose its meaning and power
      and be more and more mistreated.
Besides, after all, what would life be worth
      were love not there to brighten and better
it?

The View from the Circle Bar

I chase the madness
at the bottom of this glass,
residing in a twinkle of an eye,
        and in the shake of a tight skirt.

Tomorrow will be a huge day
in the lives of people here, as the
circle will expand, the boundary will grow
        --or maybe it will shrink.

I watch the people here in the
Circle Bar on Main St. grooving
to Marvin Gaye, getting drunk,
        trying to forget what tomorrow will bring.

Lives will go on hold
and come screeching to a halt
with the impending news
        that we are all expendable.

Discovering that one is expendable
is one of life's lowest moments.
It brings with it insecurity and anguish
        that one is not good enough.

There is a sense of dread and melancholy
that we have no purpose, no direction,
we wonder what we will do and in which
          direction our next steps will take us.

Are we paying a price for something
we did somewhere in the past,
or are we being blamed for the
          ineptness of others around and above us?

We want answers, but we aren't even sure
what the questions are or how to ask them.
We want reasons, even though we know
          that no reason is good enough.

So, we chase our fears and sadness
away by seeking the glass's bottom
and dancing away the bad karma
          of decisions gone awry.

We hide ourselves in preparation for
and lubricate our emotions against
our succumbing to the fears ahead,
          then close our eyes and pray for ignorance.

Feeling and Sensitivity

The touches that were once
warm and sensitive
are today cold
and without feeling.
The numbness slackens
and the sensations disappear,
I cannot feel the sand beneath
my toes
or the wind on
my head.
What I reach for is beyond
my grasp.
But I can hear the voices
of strangers
and the music of a
dawning reality.
A symphony of perception creeps into
my head,
but I am unaware of it.
My warmth
has lost touch with its sensitivity and
my feelings
are minus several degrees of its awareness.

A Window on Perspective

A woman sings karaoke
while I sit and drink and contemplate.
I am invalidated and angry
(even using the word "invalidated" pisses me off),
happy and exhausted,
weary and resigned.
To my right,
I look out the window and watch as, out on Wilshire,
     an old-looking middle-aged woman
     pokes through the garbage can on the corner.

I bet on the baseball playoff game
tonight and won.
A parlay on three hockey games
would have won had I had the guts
to make that bet.
I curse my cowardice
as, a half-moon hovering overhead,
I notice out the window
     an old-looking middle-aged woman
     poking through the garbage can on the
corner.

Victory and elation,
disappointment and letdown,
all relative to the beholder,
smolder like incestuous hillbillies
on a Jerry Springer show,
baring all on syndicated television,
merely to cash that virulent paycheck while,
just outside the window beside which I am sitting,
    an old-looking middle-aged woman
    pokes through the garbage can on the corner.
Shame and embarrassment
steal over me for things
I have done or said,
ways I have acted or reacted,
situations I have caused or created.
I feel sorry for myself and think that
I am the unluckiest person on earth,
until I look out that window and see
    an old-looking middle-aged woman
    poking through the garbage can on the corner.

My wife sleeps at home
while I am in this bar,
sad, alone, near the breaking point.
Cowardly and full of self-loathing,
I pine away, genuflective before a bottle
and this pen and paper,
attempting to discern my lot in life,
while outside, with no home and a sorry lot in life,
     an old-looking middle-aged woman
     pokes through the corner garbage can.

Entitlement

What is entitlement?
Is it a large bank account,
expensive house,
or fast car?
Is it race, nationality, gender, religion, or
ethnicity?
Is it a beautiful face, lean body, or hard muscles?
I don't know what it is, but I see it every day,
and, frankly,
I am sick of it.
Because of this catchword,
the lines of graciousness and acceptance of others
have been eradicated.
Every day, I experience and/or observe this
phenomenon
and I shudder at the direction in which
this country—
this world—
is headed.
Everyone seems to think he or she is entitled
to whatever it is he or she wants,
the wishes of others or the needs of the masses
be damned.

I am entitled to be rude and act ugly,
to have what I want,
to my rightful place,
because
my ancestors were repressed
or because
my ancestors were wealthy
or because
my child is a better student or athlete.
I am entitled
because
I am a woman
I am Asian
I am beautiful
I live in a Chelsea townhouse
or because
I am an Ivy Leaguer
I drive a German sports car
I am a victim
I live on 5th Avenue
or because
I am on welfare
I am black
I am fat and lazy
I am handicapped
or because
Of my ethnicity
or because
I know the Prime Minister or President
or because I…

The reasons are endless, superfluous, and disingenuous.
Why the need for entitlement?
It has done nothing but
cultivate bitterness,
promote segregation,
emphasize separation,
cause misunderstanding,
foster mistrust,
and
endanger this country's—
no, this world's—
relationships.
Because of this attitude,
our planet
is more divided than ever.
Every day brings fresh news of conflict between people
who feel that they are more
entitled to what it is they want
than are the people who believe opposite,
who also believe THEY are more
entitled to what it is they want.
It is a vicious cycle and it is not new.
No, it has been around for millennia.

However, the relentlessness of
technological advancement,
the explosion in world population,
and the heightening educating of the world
have begun to narrow the distance
between neighbors and encroach upon
the privacy of the world,
serving to make this a more urgent problem
than ever before.
It can be found on small, insignificant scales,
such as a claim to a space in line
at a coffee shop,
or it can be found on larger scales,
such as a claim to a promotion
at work,
or it can be found on the grandest scales of all,
such as the claim to land or religious monument
at home.
Entitlement has always existed,
and especially on the grandest of scales;
it is one of the reasons for war.
But it is when it starts to become an epidemic on
smaller and less large scales
that the problem of entitlement
must be addressed
and the attitudes toward and surrounding it
must be altered and
compromises must be reached.

Perhaps this entitlement is part
of Nature's course
for the universe,
but I suspect not
because we as a species of humankind
have begun to believe more and more
that we are entitled to destroying
more and more parts of Nature,
literally and figuratively,
in an effort to further our own advancement,
which, of course,
is not an advancement at all.
In trying to impose our sense of entitlement upon
Nature,
we run the risk of provoking Her wrath.
When we believe we are entitled
to know and understand
what it is that Nature
knows and understands,
so much so that we will attain this
knowledge and understanding
at any cost,
we jeopardize the future of Humankind's
relationship with Nature
and, indeed,
we jeopardize
even the future of Humankind itself.

News of End

dying footsteps
        on a
borrowed freeway.
the troops behind me
        huddled
in gathering.
the news of end
        flickering,
                waiting.

Deliquescence

Deliquescence:
A more beautiful word I've not yet found
In my native language, for the very images
It evokes in my soul's dreams are every bit
As sensual as the rolling of the word off my
tongue.

Deliquescence:
Ahh, but a brief pause causes me to realize my error:
There *is* a more beautiful formation of letters that
Can escape my trembling lips and fill my senses
with
Indescribable joy, though more than just one word,
it is:

Your name...

Her Love

Her love,
As if emanating
From the moon's beams,
Speaks to me
Placidly and passionately,
Encapsulating me in its
Sensual throes.

Her mysteries are the
Undulations of the lunar surface;
Her face is the
Radiant splendor of its reflection back to me;
Her soul is the
Incandescence of time on its formation.

I feel her eyes on me as I sleep
I feel her touch on me as I smile
I feel her tears on me as I shudder
I feel her breath on me as I sing
I feel her beauty on me as I seduce
I feel her love around me as I surrender.

It's Best Experienced for Oneself

Love is a perspective best
Experienced for oneself,
        For it is a relative matter
And is rarely the same
        To multitudes of people, nor
Even to the same person
        From moment to moment.

        To some, love is a look in one's eye,
To others, it's the texture of one's hair;
        A third might think that it's fleeting,
And a fourth takes it to be eternal.
        A fifth is all about personality,
While to a sixth all depends on physiognomy;
        Still others attribute it to sex only,
Whereas an eighth might find in it only
abstinence.

        Love is faithful and turbulent,
Tolerant and indiscreet,
        Placid and infidel,
Opinionated and clandestine,
        It is all of the above
And none of the below,
        Or below all of that which
Is none of the above:

It is an aromatic blossom
And a withered leaf;
It withstands Time
And flirts with destruction.
I can see it on a subway
Or through a café window,
Fluttering effortlessly on my shoulder,
Sending chills down my spine.
Laughing, it mocks me,
While seducing me with its benevolence.

Ahh...
Love, the master of destinies
And captor of fantasies;
The reason to breathe
And often a ransacking of logic.
It is Nature's grandest endeavor
And is best experienced for oneself.

'Tis You

Cuddled we lay
    The night so still
Our bodies so close
    To ward off the chill
In time unison
    Beat as one our hearts
Just like our souls
    The sum of all parts
'Tis you, my sweet,
    whom I chose
my mango, my dove,
    my sweet delicate rose.
May we continue to grow
    And together be old
Our love always to bloom
    Never to droop or fold

Fluttering

Pigeons flutter nightly at my room window
waking me from my dreams;
My heart flutters madly at thoughts of you
making reality from my dreams.

Contrast

You sit on steps near a street corner
selling goods to feed Your feeble body;
I sit in a pub overlooking your position,
drinking, writing, and thinking smug thoughts.
You sit, huddled and demure, shivering
and waiting for Your next customer;
I sit, bold and colorful, ruminating
and waiting for My next buzz.
You sit in your native country,
probably not too far from Your loved ones;
I sit in yet another foreign country
far from My family and loved ones.
Your thoughts are on survival
and from where will come the next meal;
My thoughts are on bacchanalia
and in which country I should imbibe next.
You sit and clean the area where You sit,
Your kind heart better than Your plight;
I sit and cleanse my mind with drink and verse,
my heart longing for kindness like Yours.
You know Your lot in life and
seem to have accepted it;
I'm not sure of My lot and
don't know what it is I should accept.
You sit
I sit

and one truth is certain:

Your way is that way—
Mine is the opposite.

One Look

It is said that self-restraint
        is the cornerstone to enlightenment;

One look at the miracle of you, however,
        and I long for infinite ignorance.

A Body of Work

A lustfulness settles in your eyes
    And sits restlessly on the curve
    Of your lovely breasts.
Your lips part in anticipation of
    What lies behind the realm of
    Expectation in your soul.
Imagination caresses your hips,
    Enthralled by the possibilities
    Of the dance there between.
Your navel is all butterflies and shivers
    At the thought of hot breath
    Tracing its edges teasingly.
Your thighs meet at a moist, tender
    Vortex that so innocently begin
    As separated feet below.
Oceans of want and longing, hidden by
    Ancient curses, bubble forth
    To the surface and consume me.

The Grain of Sand

Consider the grain of sand in its
    seaside repose.
Has any thought ever been given
    To this one of countless?
Not by me, it hadn't; that is,
    Until I saw her
Covered from torso to foot with
    Thousands of its twins.
Only then did I consider the
    Grain of sand in its repose.

Oh! How I longed to be any one
    Of those grains!
How I yearned to cling to that
    Celestial skin!
How I ached to be one with those
    Delectable curves!
How breathless I became at the thought
    Of lying amidst those glorious mysteries.
After wishing to be graced by the touch of
    A hand that brushed off those grains,
How I considered the grain of sand
    In its Elysian repose.

Love Is a Binary Star System

Love is the common center of mass
Around which two people should revolve.
They should be interdependent entities
Sharing a dependence on each other, as well.
Being separate beings and not mutually exclusive
Is a balance for which it should be strived.
Together, their individual uniqueness conspire
To equal a unique oneness between them.
Growth by each alone is advancement
By and for the whole.
Together, but individual, inspires
Freedom, acceptance, trust, understanding.
They can be seen as separate,
But by their actions, an observer can always
Infer the existence of and influence by the other.
The differences in each allow for and determine
That each will learn much from the other:
Vision is more acute, skin is more sensitive,
Life's aroma becomes more pungent;
Thought is more aware, and body more sensual.
In this relationship, individual potential is reached
While goals of the relationship are also fulfilled.
Integration of senses, minds, and thoughts—
Regardless of degree of similarity or difference—
Heightens beyond imagination or expectation
The mental pleasures and physical desires.
Without such integration, concupiscence is
mundane
And what could be deliquescent collapses.

The Pub of Transience

Pull up a stool
At the pub of transience
And rest your weary soul.
Recharge your intelligence
With a cup of candor.
Resolve your self-worth
With a pint of tolerance.
Indulge in a mug of levity
Because taking yourself too seriously
Is just another addiction.

Entrust the barkeep
To pour you a shot
Of her best caricature—
But don't react too harshly
If it doesn't suit your tastes.
After all, one woman's poison
Is another woman's ambrosia.

To some, this is a house of worship,
While others call it a den of miscreancy.
Depending upon your
Viewpoint
Preference
Inebriation,
It can be either, neither, or both.

Just as it's her right
To create as she sees fit,
It's not hers to force you to imbibe;
And just as it's your right
Not to accept her endeavour,
It's not yours to react violently.

The pub of transience
Is just that:
A public place shared
By those who cross the threshold
For only a short period of time.
It's best to partake judiciously,
Share accordingly,
Listen tolerantly,
Banter gracefully,
React graciously,
Understand rationally,
Mingle curiously
All without demanding of others
Their acceptance of your dogma.

Leave the pub as neat
As possible for those who
Come after you because,
Don't forget, you are more ephemeral
Than is the pub of transience.

Encroaching Rhythms

What is the rhythm
that awakens our primordial ego?
If we concede life
to our final breath,
does this mean that existence,
as we know it, ceases?
Should we really care if
this is a questioned unanswered?
How about if we simply
just enjoy the life we have
in the only way we know
that works for us,
but without creating vibes that
manipulate those around us?
In an ever-encroaching world,
is such a thing possible?

Aroma of the World

The aroma of the world wafts by on an
Unearthly plane,
Not of candlelight and alkaline,
But of buffalo-hide and quinine.
We kiss the fish-tinged night of ecstasy
With our alcohol-soaked fingertips.
Tomorrow is a yet-unattainable memory
Of countless thousands of sober yesterdays.
Unfathomable tongues of a reversible language
Mix with the music of Simon and Garfunkel
And the ever-understandable tongue of
The world's most popular sport.
It's a night of endless copulation,
Football observance, and vigilance of the soul.

Ourselves Lost

Sublime are the curves of
      Matter all around us;
Divergent are the currents that
      Assail our senses;
Existential are the drinks
      Poured into our voids;
Implausible are the thoughts
      Our guilt avoids;
Immaculate is our ice
      Untouched by thoughtfulness;
Incandescent is the emotion of
      One unafraid to experience;
Fervent is our seeming need
      To avoid abject loneliness;
Unnecessary is our need to embellish
      Our dependence on "progress";
Unavailable become our souls
      Toward what is natural;
And lost becomes our sense of
      Worth, purpose, right, and wrong.

Damadola

Bones, psyches, and lives decimated
As guided bombs land and shred.
Flesh, homes, and sanity destroyed
As hope and quietude shatter.
Another senseless campaign of hell
Backed up by arrogant excuse
And unprovoked imperial abuse.
To the world, twill be hard to sell
The mad, unforgivable error
That befell tiny, remote Damadola
On behalf of God, pop, and Coca-Cola
In this stage of "War on Terror."
Attempts to explain it away
Show an absence of sentience,
An utter lack of civilised conscience
As survivors look on with dismay.
From all corners, should there be heard
Deafening cries of condemnation
So any future duplication
Will safely be deterred.

A Collection of Haikus

Mood
A cloudy day dawns—
A reflection of my thoughts,
But not of my heart

Meditation
I hear particles
Dance on mushroom caps—or do
I hallucinate?

Gales
Sunbeam falls from grace
And Raindrop rebounds from sin
Wind? It does neither.

Time
Seconds blink by me
Observing a relative
Rhythm oft ignored

Knowledge
Education is
Not confined only to school—
It involves life, too.

Enlightenment
Enlightenment—what
A concept! Except, these days,
Of it, most have none.

Waiting
A typhoon rolls in
Unobstructed, like a shark
Licking you awake.

Foreplay
Pearl-juiced labia
Pink folds of heavenly bliss—
My unblinking queen.

Coitus
Soft, unctuous, wet—
Pulsing, ready for my jet;
Once in, I am set.

Language
What is language? A
Harbinger of one's thoughts, or
A molder of them?

Languages
If one knows two or
More, thoughts have more than one well
From which to spring

Soccer
Inspiration for
All, save one, it links rivals
And strengthens bonds

Soccer 2
A beautiful game
For those who live it, minced shame
For the ignorant.

Beach
Waves gently breaking,
Wind kicking, sand blowing in—
Aaahh! Beach beckonings!

Beckonings
Sunburned neck and back
Aching muscles, umbrella smashed—
Aahhhh! Beach beckonings!

Fall
The distance beckons,
Leaves changing like ice in a
Martini tumbler.

Conundrum
What is sustenance—
That which sustains or maintains?
Or a moon that wanes?

Release
Through drink, the real mind
Reveals its stark beauty, ire,
And primality